HANDY CRAFTS

BEADS 'N' BADGES

Gillian Souter

Gareth Stevens Publishing
A WORLD ALMANAC EDUCATION GROUP COMPANY

★ Before You Start ★

Some of these projects can get messy, so make sure your work area is covered with newspaper. For projects that need paint, you can use acrylic paint, poster paint, or any other kind of paint that is labeled nontoxic. Ask an adult to help you find paints that are safe to use and to help with some of the projects that require sewing. You will also need an adult's help to make some of the projects, especially for cutting with a craft knife or using the oven for baking.

Please visit our web site at: www.garethstevens.com
For a free color catalog describing Gareth Stevens' list of high-quality books and multimedia programs, call 1-800-542-2595 (USA) or 1-800-461-9120 (Canada).
Gareth Stevens Publishing's Fax: (414) 332-3567.

Library of Congress Cataloging-in-Publication Data

Souter, Gillian
    Beads 'n' Badges / by Gillian Souter
      p. cm. -- (Handy crafts)
    Includes bibliographical references and index.
    ISBN 0-8368-2819-4 (lib. bdg.)
    1. Handicraft. [1. Beads. 2. Beadwork. 3. Jewelry making.
    4. Badges. 5. Handicraft.] I. Series.
    TT160 .S65 2001
    745.5--dc21   00-052245

This U.S. edition first published in 2001 by
Gareth Stevens Publishing
A World Almanac Education Group Company
330 West Olive Street, Suite 100
Milwaukee, Wisconsin 53212 USA

This U.S. edition © 2001 by Gareth Stevens, Inc. Original edition published as *Beads and Badges* in 1999 by Off the Shelf Publishing, 32 Thomas Street, Lewisham NSW 2049, Australia. Text, projects, and layout © 1999 by Off the Shelf Publishing. Additional end matter © 2001 by Gareth Stevens, Inc.

Illustrations: Clare Watson
Photographs: Andre Martin
Cover design: Joel Bucaro
Gareth Stevens editor: Monica Rausch

Printed in the United States of America

1 2 3 4 5 6 7 8 9 05 04 03 02 01

Contents

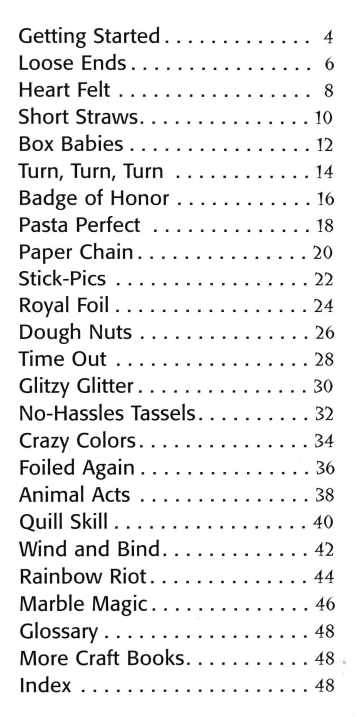

Getting Started

You can make your own beads and badges from all sorts of things. Here are some items you can use.

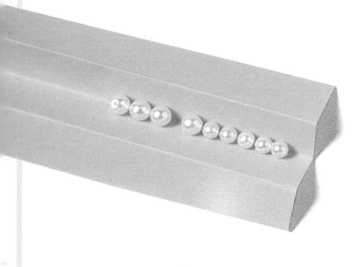

Fold a piece of paper back and forth and use it to arrange beads before you thread them onto a string.

You can find special parts for making jewelry in a craft store. These parts are called *findings*.

Use an old egg carton to sort beads by shape or size.

You can string beads onto any strong thread. Embroidery floss is both strong and colorful, and elastic is perfect for making bracelets.

You will need lots of large safety pins if you plan to make badges.

Look around your home and collect things that might be useful. Look for interesting buttons, colorful candy wrappers, snippets of ribbon and yarn, and scraps of gift wrap.

Loose Ends

Here are a few tips for making beads and badges.

Make sure the thread for your necklace or bracelet is long enough to fit over your head or hand. Allow extra thread to tie a knot.

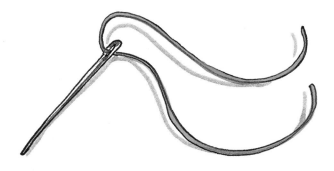

Use a needle to string beads on a strong piece of cord or a double length of thread. Strong thread will keep the strand of beads from breaking.

A twisted cord works well with large beads. To make this cord, twist a very long piece of embroidery floss over and over. Then hold the ends tight and fold the floss in half, letting the two halves slowly twist together.

When you are painting or varnishing beads, hold each bead with a toothpick. Stick the toothpick in corrugated cardboard or a lump of clay while the beads dry.

Tie the ends of a string of beads in an overhand knot (as shown).

You can tape a large safety pin on the back of most badges. For badges made of felt or other fabric, you will need to sew on the pin. Make sure you tape or sew on the unmovable bar of the safety pin, so the pin can be opened easily.

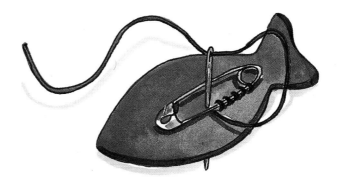

7

Heart Felt

Here's a heart felt badge you can make with lots of love!

1 Draw a shape on scrap paper. Cut out the shape.

2 Lay the paper shape on a piece of felt. Cut the felt neatly around the shape.

3 Lay the felt shape on another color of felt. Cut out a slightly larger shape around it. Repeat this step several times, using the largest felt shape each time to cut out even larger felt shapes.

4 Thread a needle with strong thread. Sew the unmovable bar of a large safety pin onto the back of the largest felt shape. You may need to ask an adult to help you with the sewing.

5 Stack the shapes in order of size, with the largest shape on the bottom and the safety pin on the back. Stitch through all the layers of felt several times to hold them together.

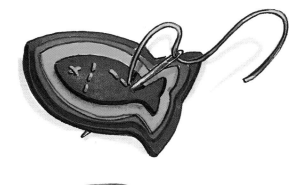

★ **Bright Idea** ★
Try using different shapes of felt to make a badge like the one below.

Short Straws

These simple straw beads are a snap — so string a double strand!

:::::::::::::::::::::::::::::::::::::
You Will Need
- scissors
- plastic drinking straws
- cotton thread
- needle
:::::::::::::::::::::::::::::::::::::

1 Cut colorful plastic drinking straws into short pieces. The pieces can be all the same size or different sizes.

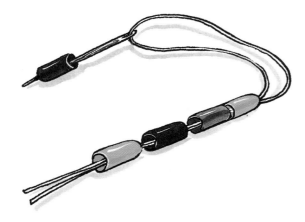

2 Cut cotton thread to two times the length of your necklace. Thread a needle halfway along the thread to make a double strand of thread. String the straw beads. Repeat this step to make two matching strands.

3 At each end of the two strands, tie the four threads together in an overhand knot.

4 Thread a needle with a short piece of thread. Tie a knot on the thread's end. Ask an adult to pierce a small straw bead through its side and string it on. String two more beads in the normal way, through the straw's openings.

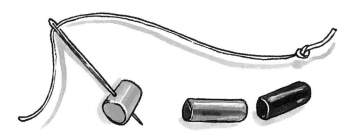

5 Repeat step 4 two more times to make three short strands. Tie the ends of the short strands onto the middle of the two long strands.

★ Bright Idea ★
Twist the two long strands of beads before tying their ends together.

Box Babies

Matchbox badges can hold lots of surprises. A spider and a doll are just two ideas. Can you think of more?

You Will Need
- scissors
- pipe cleaner
- colored felt
- glue
- marker
- tape
- two matchboxes
- paints and paintbrush
- two safety pins

1 To make a spider, cut a long pipe cleaner into three pieces. Bend one piece into an **M** shape. Wrap the other pieces around the middle of the **M** to form six legs. Spiders have eight legs, but this spider doesn't need that many!

2 To make a doll, draw the shape of a head and body on pink felt and draw the shapes of a bonnet and dress on green felt. Cut out the shapes. Glue the dress and bonnet onto the doll. Use a marker to make two dots for eyes. Cut a square of blue felt for a pillow.

12

3 Tape one leg of the spider to the bottom of a matchbox. Glue the felt doll into another matchbox.

4 Paint the matchbox covers, then let the paint dry. Tape a safety pin on the back of each cover.

5 Put glue on the back of each matchbox. Slide the boxes into their covers, but leave the boxes slightly open. Let the glue dry.

★ **Bright Idea** ★
Make a felt mouse for your matchbox.

13

Turn, Turn, Turn

Use old gift wrap to create something new when you make these beautiful beads.

1 Cut a piece of wrapping paper 12 inches (30 centimeters) long. Draw lines on the paper to make paper strips that are wider at one end than at the other.

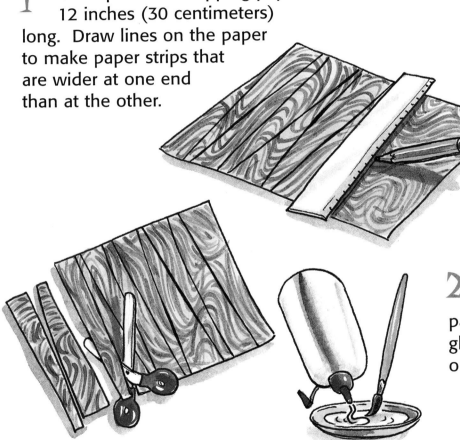

2 Cut out the paper strips. Use a paintbrush to mix white glue with a little water on a plate.

3 Lay the wide end of a paper strip along the side of a pencil. Turn the pencil to roll the strip around it.

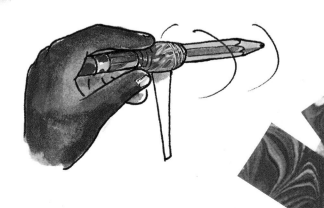

14

4 Keep rolling until you reach the narrow end of the strip. Brush glue onto the end and press it down to make a tightly coiled bead.

5 Slide the bead off the pencil. Brush the white glue mixture over it, then stand the bead upright on scrap paper to dry. Repeat steps 3, 4, and 5 to make more beads, then string the beads on a cord.

★ Bright Idea ★
You can make small beads using straight, narrow paper strips.

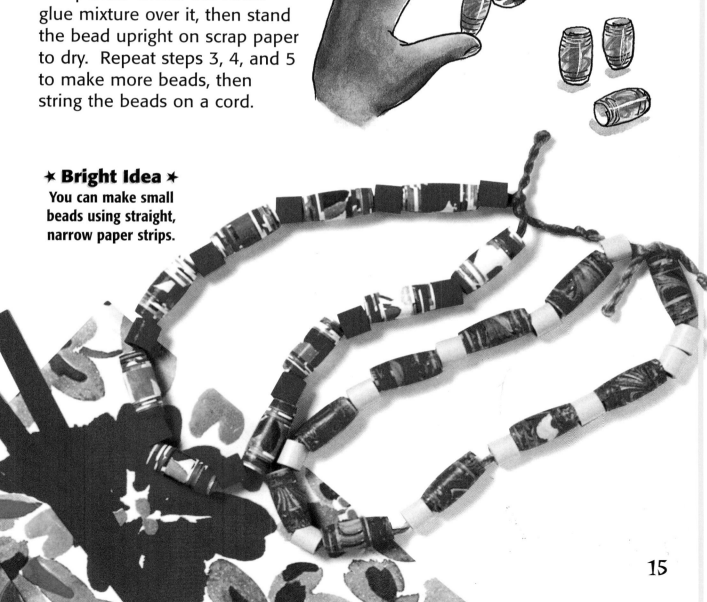

15

Badge of Honor

Reward your friends with this great medal of honor.

1 Use a large coin to draw two circles on thin cardboard. Cut out the circles.

2 Cover one side of each cardboard circle with a piece of aluminum foil, folding the foil edges over the circle's back.

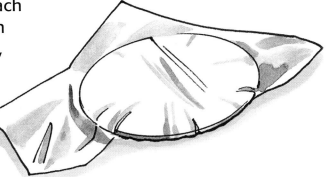

3 Use a blunt pencil to draw or write on the front of each circle.

16

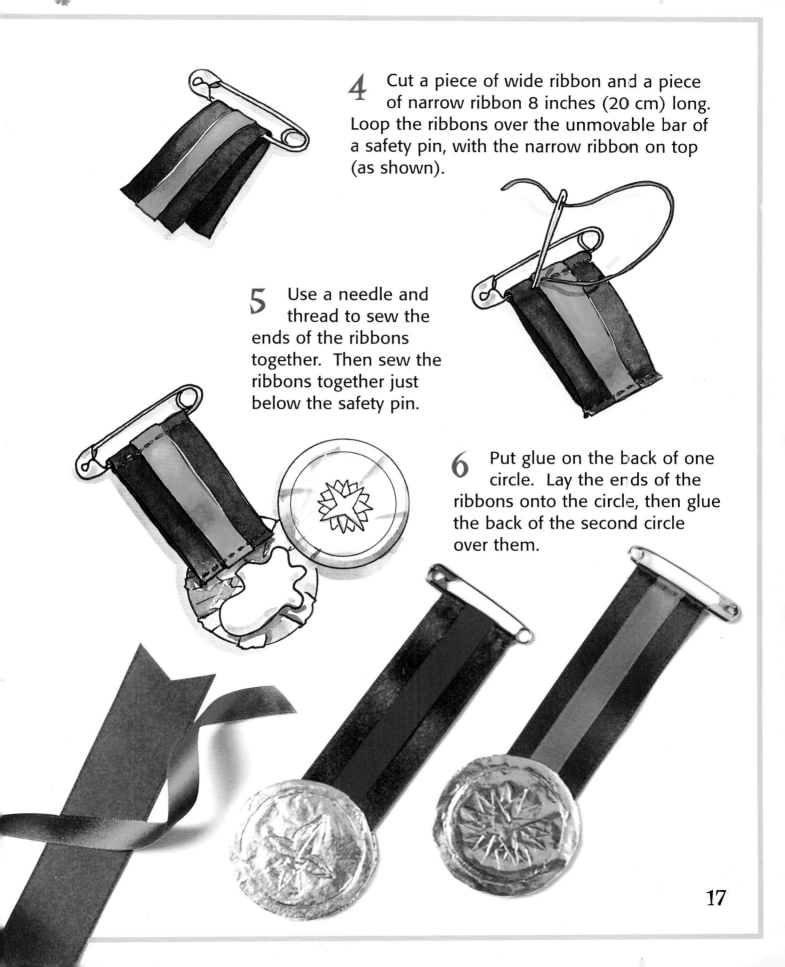

4 Cut a piece of wide ribbon and a piece of narrow ribbon 8 inches (20 cm) long. Loop the ribbons over the unmovable bar of a safety pin, with the narrow ribbon on top (as shown).

5 Use a needle and thread to sew the ends of the ribbons together. Then sew the ribbons together just below the safety pin.

6 Put glue on the back of one circle. Lay the ends of the ribbons onto the circle, then glue the back of the second circle over them.

17

Pasta Perfect

Neat noodle shapes are perfect for nifty necklaces.

1 Pour a small amount of water into several glasses. Add ten drops of a different color of food coloring to each glass.

2 Drop a few noodles into each glass. Stir the noodles with a fork for about 30 seconds.

18

3   Use a fork to lift the noodles out of the glasses. Let most of the colored water drip off of the noodles, then lay them on scrap paper to dry.

4   When the noodles are dry, thread them onto a piece of string to make a necklace or a bracelet.

5   For noodles that are not hollow, tie a short piece of string around each noodle, then tie the string onto the necklace.

Paper Chain

These colorful paper chains are stretchy and strong!

1   Use a pencil and ruler to draw lines
    ½ inch (13 millimeters) apart on
colored paper. Cut out strips of
paper along the lines.

2   Glue together the
    ends of two different
colored strips to form
a large **L** shape.

3 Fold the top strip over
the glued ends. Fold
the side strip across. Keep
folding the strips over and
across each other.

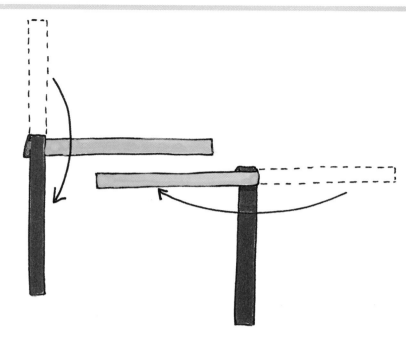

4 When you get near the end
of a strip, glue another strip
onto the end and keep folding.

5 When the chain is long enough
to fit over your head or hand,
glue down the last fold. Trim off
any extra paper. Glue together
the two ends of the chain to
make a bracelet or necklace.

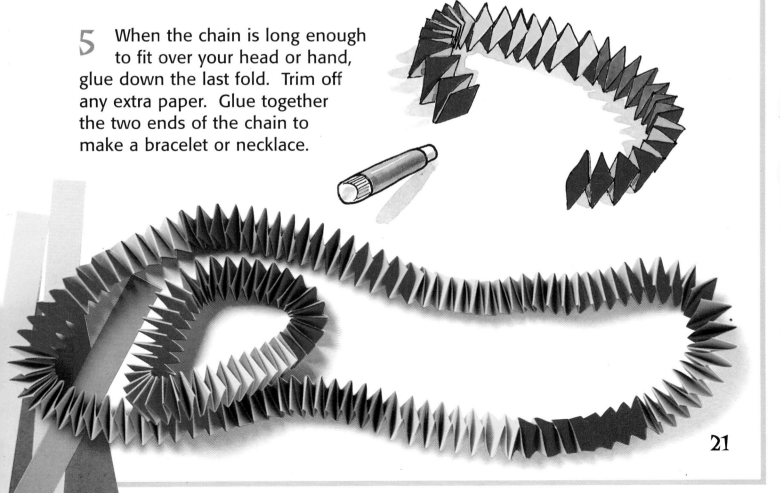

21

Stick-Pics

Here's a way to wear your funny photographs on a fantastic badge.

You Will Need

- scissors
- photograph that can be cut up
- clear plastic bottle
- paints and paintbrush
- white glue
- safety pin
- tape

1 Cut out part of a photograph of a friend or a pet. Make sure no one minds that you are cutting up the photograph!

2 Cut out two pieces of clear plastic from a large plastic bottle. The pieces should be the same size and shape.

3 On one piece of plastic, paint a border for your photo. Paint small details first. Let the paint dry, then paint over it with a background color.

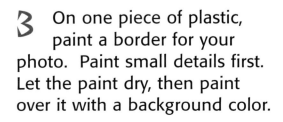

4 When the paint is dry, lay the photograph face down on the painted plastic, centering the photograph in the border. Glue the second piece of plastic onto the back of the photo and painted plastic.

5 Let the glue dry. Tape a safety pin on the back of the second piece of plastic.

★ **Helpful Hint** ★
Curved plastic gives
the badge a 3-D look.

Royal Foil

These sparkling badges are sure to make a splash.

You Will Need

- pencil and scissors
- corrugated cardboard
- white glue and water
- bowl
- newspaper
- paintbrush
- paints
- foil candy wrappers
- safety pin
- tape

1 Draw a shape on cardboard, then cut out the shape. This shape will be your badge.

2 Mix equal amounts of white glue and water in a bowl.

3 Tear some newspaper into narrow strips. Soak each strip in the glue mixture, then lay it on the cardboard shape, overlapping strips as you go. Cover the shape with several layers of strips, then let the newspaper strips dry.

4 Your cardboard shape is now ready to become a badge. Paint the entire badge white. When the white paint is dry, paint the badge another color.

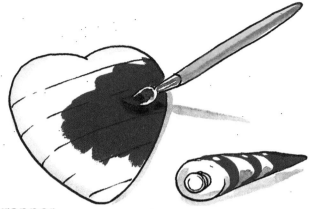

5 Roll up a foil candy wrapper and twist it into a small ring. Glue the ring onto the badge. Repeat this step to make more rings.

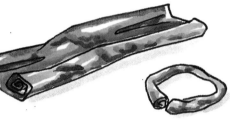

6 Roll foil wrappers into balls to fit inside the rings, then glue each ball in place. Tape a large safety pin to the back of the badge.

★ Bright Idea ★
If you don't have foil wrappers, use aluminum foil.

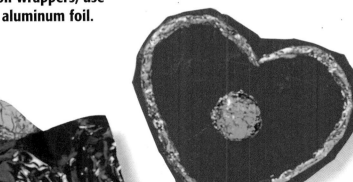

25

Dough Nuts

Create lots of crazy colored beads with simple salt dough.

1   Mix flour and salt in a bowl. Slowly stir in water and mix until a soft dough forms. Knead the dough with your hands until it is smooth.

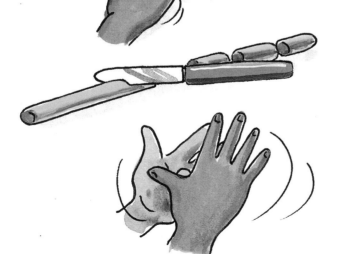

2   To make long beads, roll some dough into a long sausage shape. Slice the "sausage" into pieces of equal size. To make a round bead, roll a piece of dough between your palms.

26

3 Use a knitting needle to make a large hole in each bead. The hole will shrink slightly when the bead is baked.

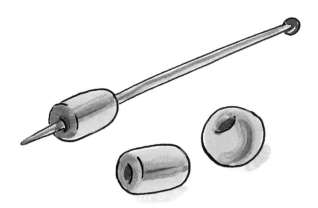

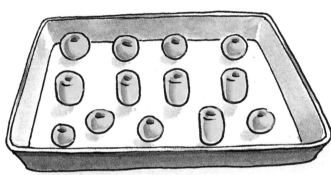

4 Place the beads upright on a cookie sheet. Ask an adult to preheat the oven to 350° Fahrenheit (180° Celsius). Bake the beads for 30 minutes.

5 Let the beads cool, then paint a base coat on each bead. When this paint is dry, paint on details.

★ Helpful Hint ★
These beads are heavy, so string them on strong thread.

Time Out

Time will fly by on this cool clock badge.

1 Using a black marker, draw a circle on white cardboard around the rim of a glass.

2 Write the number twelve at the top of the circle. Write numbers one to eleven, evenly spaced, around the circle. Cut the cardboard just outside the circle.

3 To make clock hands, cut a large and a small teardrop shape out of black cardboard.

28

4 Use a large needle to make a hole in the wide end of each clock hand. Make a hole in the center of the circle, or clock face.

5 Push a paper fastener through the holes in the clock hands and the face, then bend back the fastener's ends.

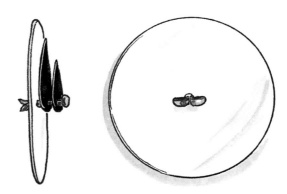

6 Glue the clock onto black cardboard. Cut a large circle around the clock face to make a black border. Tape a safety pin on the clock's back.

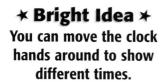
★ Bright Idea ★
You can move the clock hands around to show different times.

29

Glitzy Glitter

Anyone can wear these eye-catching earrings — you don't even need pierced ears!

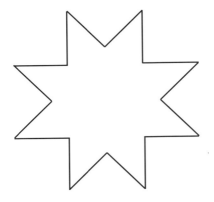

1 Lay tracing paper over the star pattern above. Use a soft pencil to trace the pattern, then turn the paper over onto thin cardboard and draw over your pencil lines. You will need four cardboard stars for one pair of earrings.

2 Cut out each cardboard star by cutting inward along each point of the star, toward the star's center. Cut two pieces of thread long enough to loop around the outside of your ear.

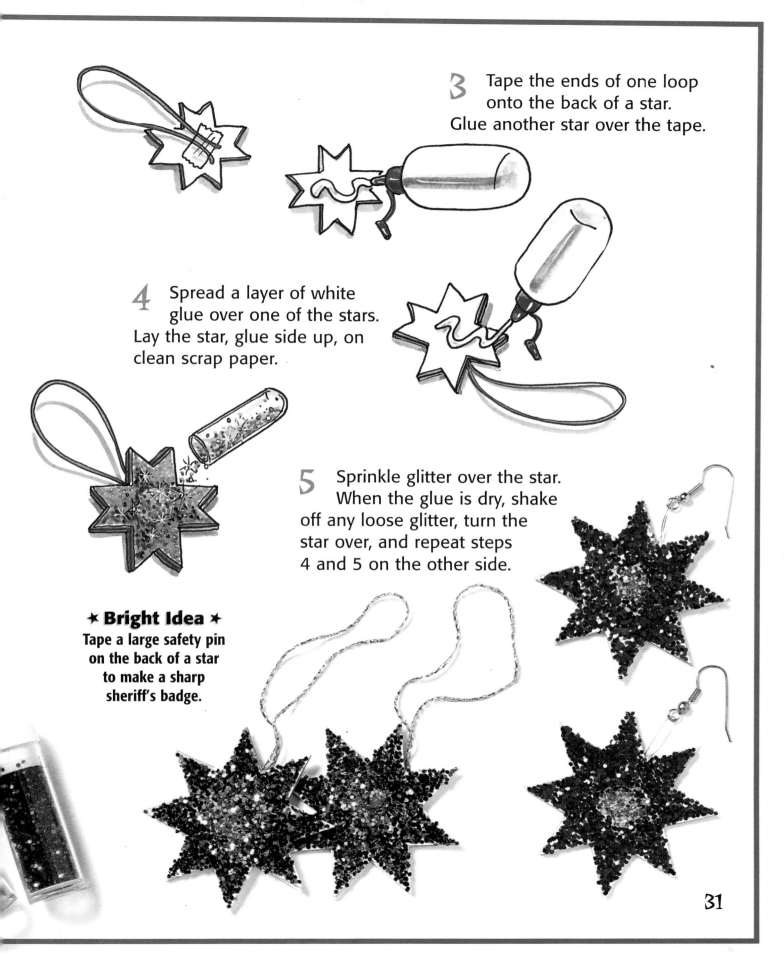

3 Tape the ends of one loop onto the back of a star. Glue another star over the tape.

4 Spread a layer of white glue over one of the stars. Lay the star, glue side up, on clean scrap paper.

5 Sprinkle glitter over the star. When the glue is dry, shake off any loose glitter, turn the star over, and repeat steps 4 and 5 on the other side.

★ **Bright Idea** ★
Tape a large safety pin on the back of a star to make a sharp sheriff's badge.

No-Hassles Tassels

You Will Need
- scissors
- ruler
- cardboard
- embroidery floss
- needle
- beads

These terrific tassels add a touch of class to a string of beads.

1 Cut out a 1 ½-inch (4-cm) square of cardboard. Wind embroidery floss around it twenty-five times.

2 Pull a short piece of embroidery floss under the loops of wound floss and tie it in a knot. Slip the loops off the cardboard.

3 Near the tied end of the loops, wind a piece of floss around the loops and tie it in a knot. Cut the bottoms of the loops to make a tassel.

4   Use a needle to string beads onto a double strand of floss. Tie a knot at each end of the strand to keep the beads in place.

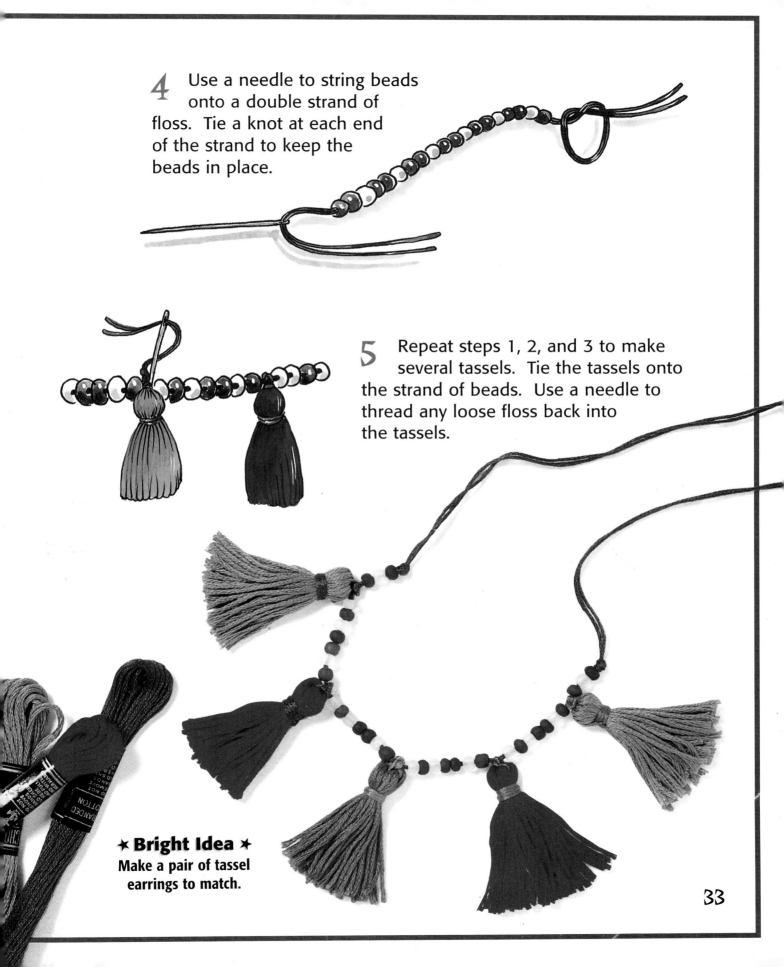

5   Repeat steps 1, 2, and 3 to make several tassels. Tie the tassels onto the strand of beads. Use a needle to thread any loose floss back into the tassels.

★ **Bright Idea** ★
Make a pair of tassel earrings to match.

33

Crazy Colors

Weave colored cardboard into weird and wacky patterns you can wear.

You Will Need
- scissors
- colored cardboard
- pencil
- white glue
- stiff cardboard
- tape
- safety pin

1 Cut out a square of colored cardboard. Draw a pencil line along one side of the square (as shown).

2 Make several cuts into the cardboard, just up to the pencil line. The cuts can be straight, wavy, or zigzag.

3 Cut another color of cardboard into straight strips. Weave one of these strips under and over the square's strips.

34

4 Weave another strip over and under the square's strips, just opposite of the first strip. Push the strips up to the pencil line. Continue weaving in strips until the square is complete.

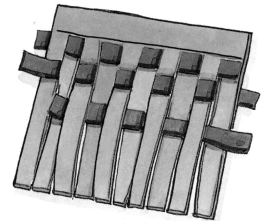

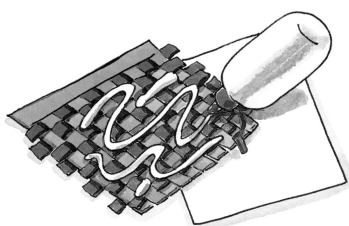

5 Spread glue over the back of the woven square. Glue the square onto a piece of stiff cardboard.

6 Cut the square into any shape you like and tape a safety pin on its back.

★ **Bright Idea** ★
Brush varnish over your badge to protect it.

Foiled Again

You Will Need
- scissors
- ruler
- aluminum foil
- paints and paintbrush or markers
- large needle
- thread

These glittering beads will make a glamorous necklace.

1 For large beads, cut out several 4-inch (10-cm) squares of foil. For small beads, cut out 2-inch (5-cm) squares.

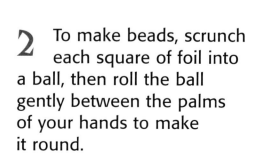

2 To make beads, scrunch each square of foil into a ball, then roll the ball gently between the palms of your hands to make it round.

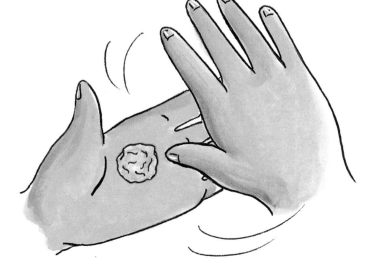

3 Stick a needle into a bead to hold the bead while you paint it. Set the painted bead on a scrap of foil to dry. You can leave some beads unpainted.

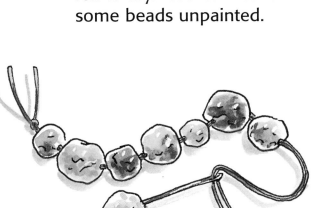

4 Use the needle to string the beads on a double length of thread. Tie a knot at each end of the strand of beads to keep the beads in place.

★ **Bright Idea** ★
Instead of using paint, try coloring the dull side of the foil with markers before you make the beads.

Animal Acts

You Will Need

- scrap paper
- pencil
- glass
- scissors
- colored felt
- needle and thread
- safety pin
- batting

These furry felt friends will bring a smile to anyone's face.

1   On scrap paper, draw a circle around the rim of a glass, then cut out the circle. Lay it on black felt and use it as a template to cut out two felt circles.

2   To make eyes, ears, and other details, cut out shapes from scraps of felt.

3   With a needle and thread, sew the shapes onto a black felt circle to make a face.

38

4 Sew a large safety pin onto the second felt circle. Lay the two felt circles together with the face on the front and the pin at the back.

5 Sew the circles together, stitching around the sides but leaving an opening. Stuff batting through the opening, then sew the opening shut.

★ **Helpful Hint** ★
Ask an adult to help you with the sewing.

Quill Skill

With quilled paper, you can create dramatic designs.

1 Using a pencil and a ruler, draw lines ½ inch (1 cm) apart on a piece of colored paper that is 12 inches (30 cm) long. Cut along the lines to make paper strips.

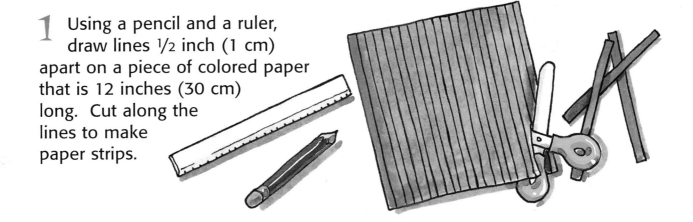

2 Hold one end of a strip on a wooden skewer. Turn the skewer to roll the paper around it. Continue rolling until you reach the end of the strip.

3 Slide the rolled strip off the skewer. Release the end and let the roll unwind to the size of a quarter. Glue down the end of the strip to keep the size of the loose roll.

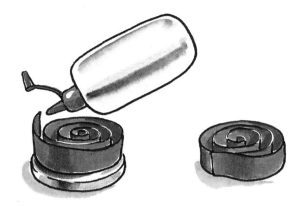

4 Pinch one side of the roll between two fingers to make a teardrop shape. You just quilled a paper strip. To quill more strips, repeat steps 2, 3, and 4.

5 Arrange the quilled strips in a pattern on a piece of cardboard, then glue them in place. Tape a safety pin on the back of the cardboard.

★ Bright Idea ★
To make different shapes, pinch the rolled strips twice – or not at all!

Wind and Bind

You Will Need

- scissors
- scrap paper
- ruler
- felt
- needle
- embroidery floss
- wooden skewer
- glue

These wonderful beads are bright, light, and easy to wind.

1 Cut a strip of paper ½ inch (13 mm) wide and 2 inches (5 cm) long. Use this strip as a template to cut out several strips of felt. Thread a needle with embroidery floss.

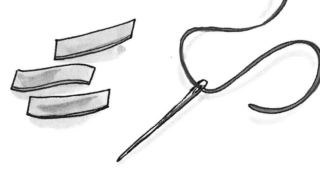

2 Hold one end of a felt strip on a wooden skewer. Turn the skewer to roll the felt around it. Continue rolling until you reach the end of the strip.

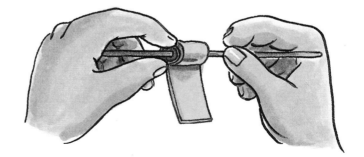

42

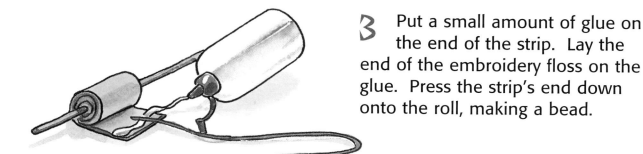

3 Put a small amount of glue on the end of the strip. Lay the end of the embroidery floss on the glue. Press the strip's end down onto the roll, making a bead.

4 Wind the embroidery floss around the felt bead. Then push the needle under the wound floss. Cut off the floss and slide the bead off the skewer. To make more beads, repeat steps 2, 3, and 4.

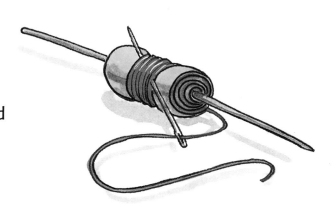

★ **Bright Idea** ★
Try winding two or more colors of floss around the felt.

Rainbow Riot

This bright, bold badge will bring a rainbow of colors to a rainy day.

1 Trace around the rims of the glasses to draw two circles, one inside the other, on cardboard. Using a ruler, draw a straight line to divide the circles in half.

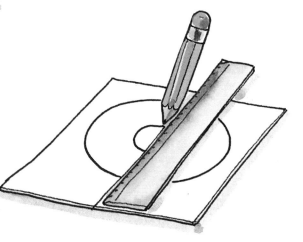

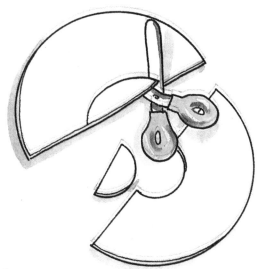

2 Cut out the large circle. Cut the circles in half along the straight line, then cut out the small half-circles, or semicircles. Now you have two rainbow shapes.

44

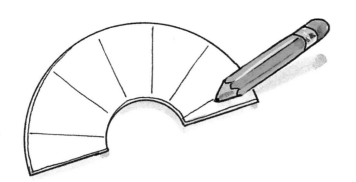

3 Draw five evenly spaced lines on one rainbow shape, to create seven sections (as shown).

4 Glue the end of a piece of embroidery floss near the shape's lower edge. Wind the floss around the cardboard, overlapping floss along the inside curve. Wind a new color in each section.

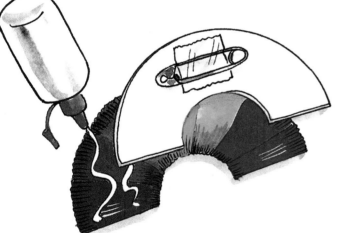

5 Each time you change colors, glue down the ends of the old and new floss on the same side of the rainbow. When the rainbow is complete, glue the second rainbow shape on the back. Tape a safety pin on the shape's back.

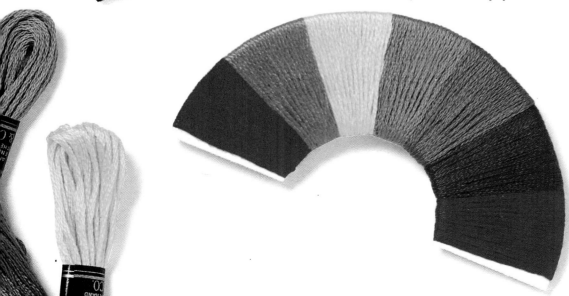

★ **Bright Idea** ★
You can also try using paints or markers to color your rainbow.

45

Marble Magic

**Make marvelous marbled beads
with two colors of clay.**

1 Knead each color of
clay in your hands until
it is soft. Roll each piece
into a long sausage shape.

You Will Need
- blue and white
  modeling clay
- dull knife
- skewer
- cookie sheet
- needle and thread

★ **Bright Idea** ★
**Try twisting three
colors of clay together.**

2 Twist the two "sausages"
of clay together. Fold this
large sausage in half and roll
the two halves together.

3 Use a dull knife
to cut the roll of
clay into pieces. Hold
each piece by the
ends and twist it.

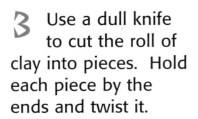

46

4 Push the ends of each piece together, then roll it into a ball between your palms.

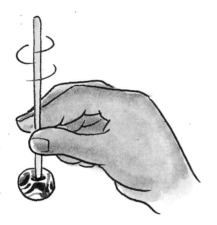

5 Drill a hole into each ball by twisting a skewer gently between your fingers. Put the beads on a cookie sheet and ask an adult to bake the clay beads in the oven, following the instructions on the clay's package. When the beads are cool, sort them according to size.

6 Using a needle and thread, string the beads, with the largest beads in the middle of the strand and the smallest beads on the ends. Tie a knot at each end of the strand.

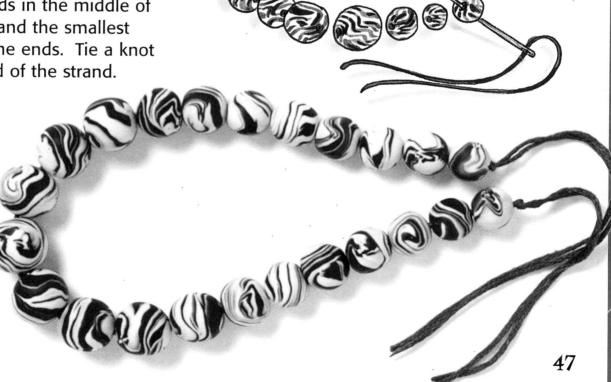

47

Glossary

batting: material made of cotton or polyester fibers and used to fill pillows or to pad quilts; stuffing.

coiled: rolled into a spiral shape.

cord: strong string usually made of several strands of thread or yarn.

corrugated: having a wrinkled surface or a surface of ridges and grooves.

embroidery floss: thick string made of several strands of thread. It is used to stitch designs on fabric.

hollow: having a hole or an empty space inside.

knead: to press or squeeze with the hands over and over.

overlap: to rest one object on top of another.

quill: (v) to roll up paper strips to make a design.

skewer: a pointed stick used to hold meat together while the meat is roasting.

strand: string or rope; a long, narrow object resembling string or rope.

template: a pattern or guide used to make copies of the pattern's shape.

varnish: a sticky, paintlike substance spread over a surface to give it a hard, shiny appearance.

weave: to create an object by passing strips of material over and under one another.

More Craft Books by Gareth Stevens

Costume Crafts. Worldwide Crafts (series). Iain MacLeod-Brudenell

Crafty Badges. Crafty Kids (series). Petra Boase

Crafty Puppets. Crafty Kids (series). Thomasina Smith

The Kids' Multicultural Art Book. Williamson Kids Can!® (series). Alexandra M. Terzian

Index

48